Burlington, Vermont in 64 Colors

Colored pencil drawings

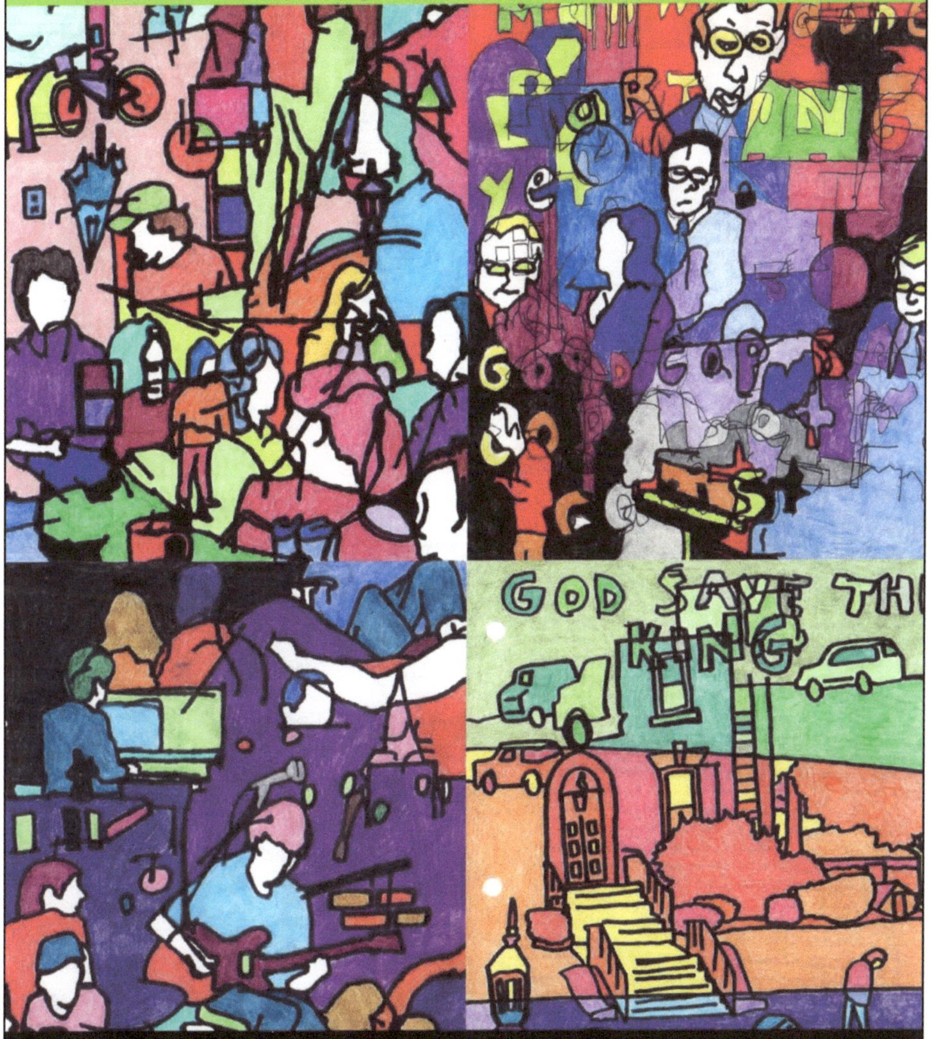

STEPHEN ALAJAJIAN

Burlington, Vermont in 64 Colors (2007-2008)

Colored pencil drawings

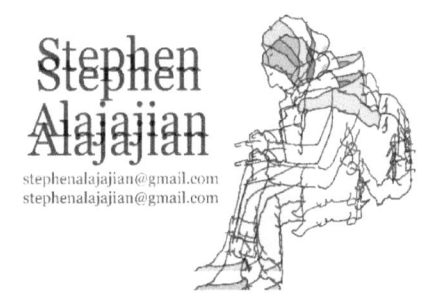

Stephen Alajajian
stephenalajajian@gmail.com
stephenalajajian@gmail.com

Published August 2019

Dedicated to Michael Martin

Dedicated to Michael Martin

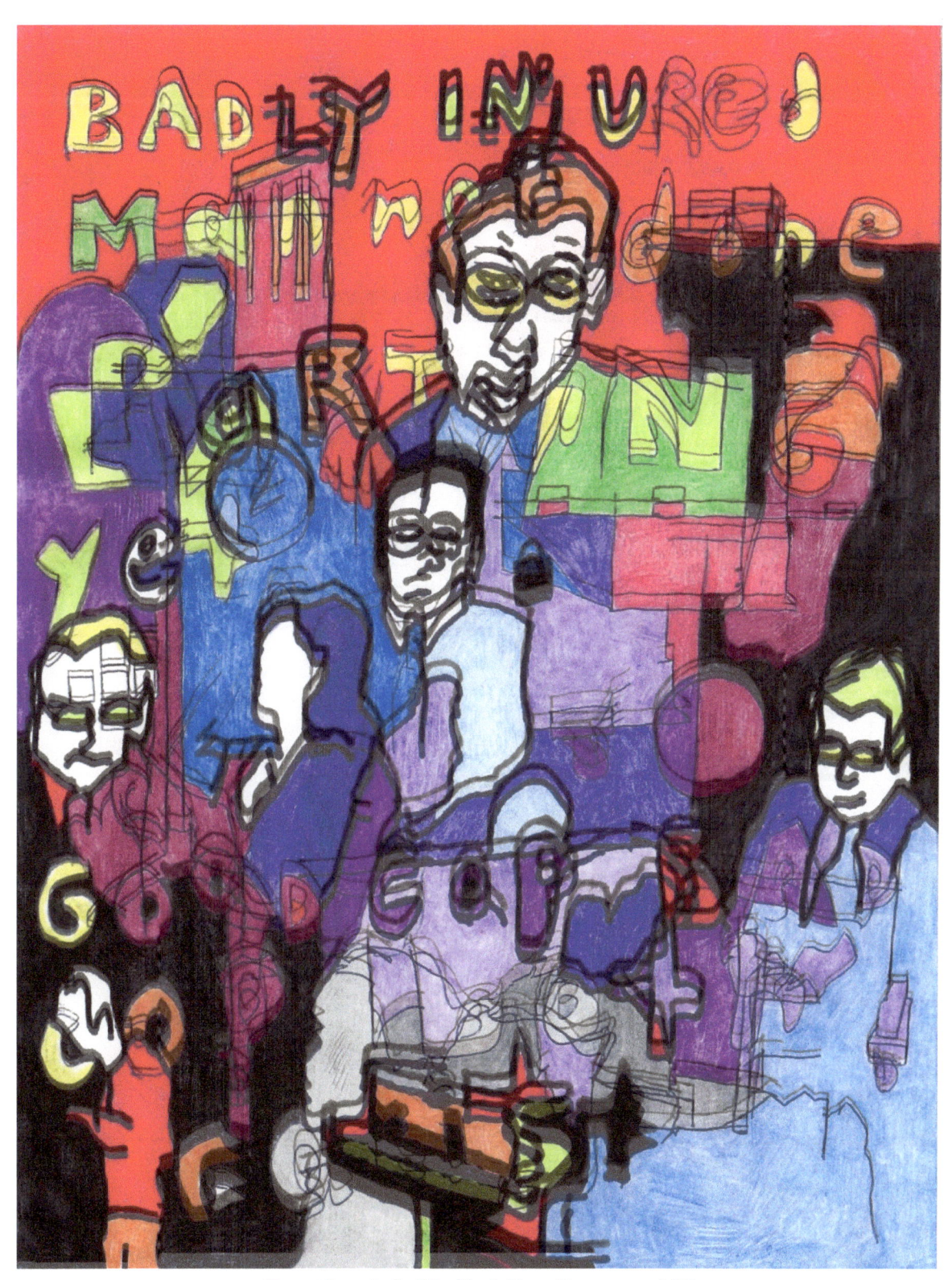

Southwick Hall / Burlington, VT

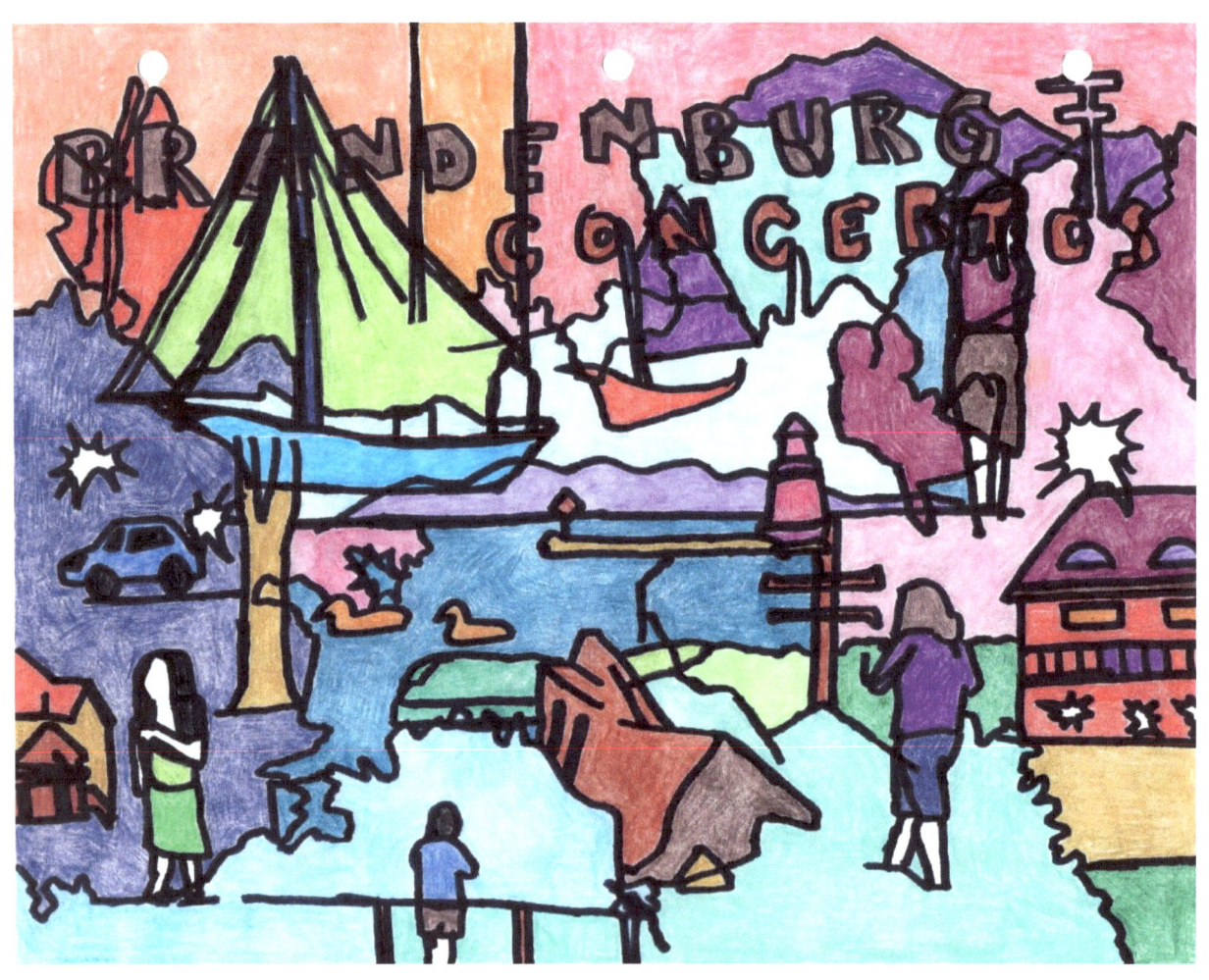

Waterfront Park No. 1 / *Burlington, VT*

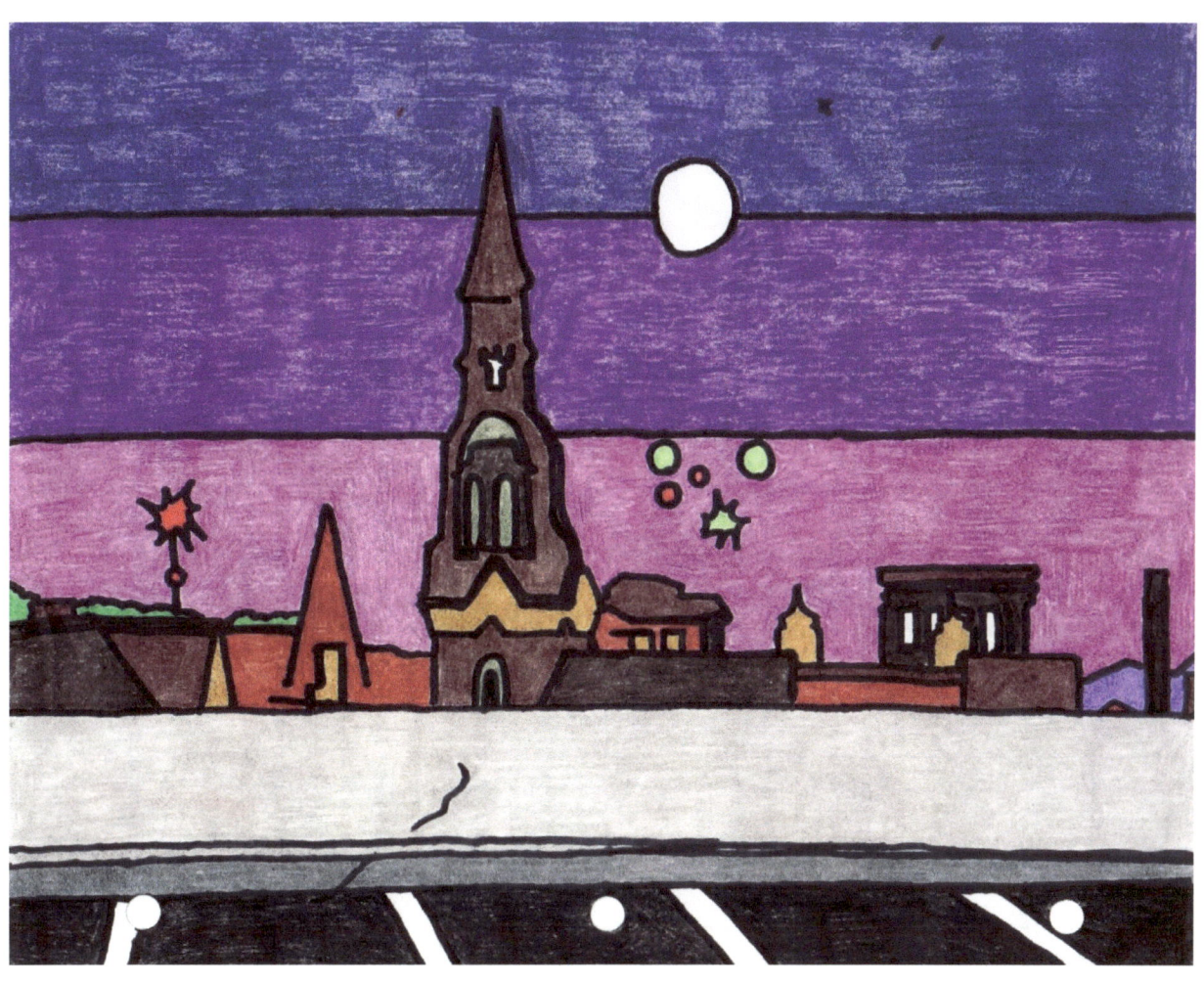

S. Winooski Ave. Parking Garage No. 1 / *Burlington, VT*

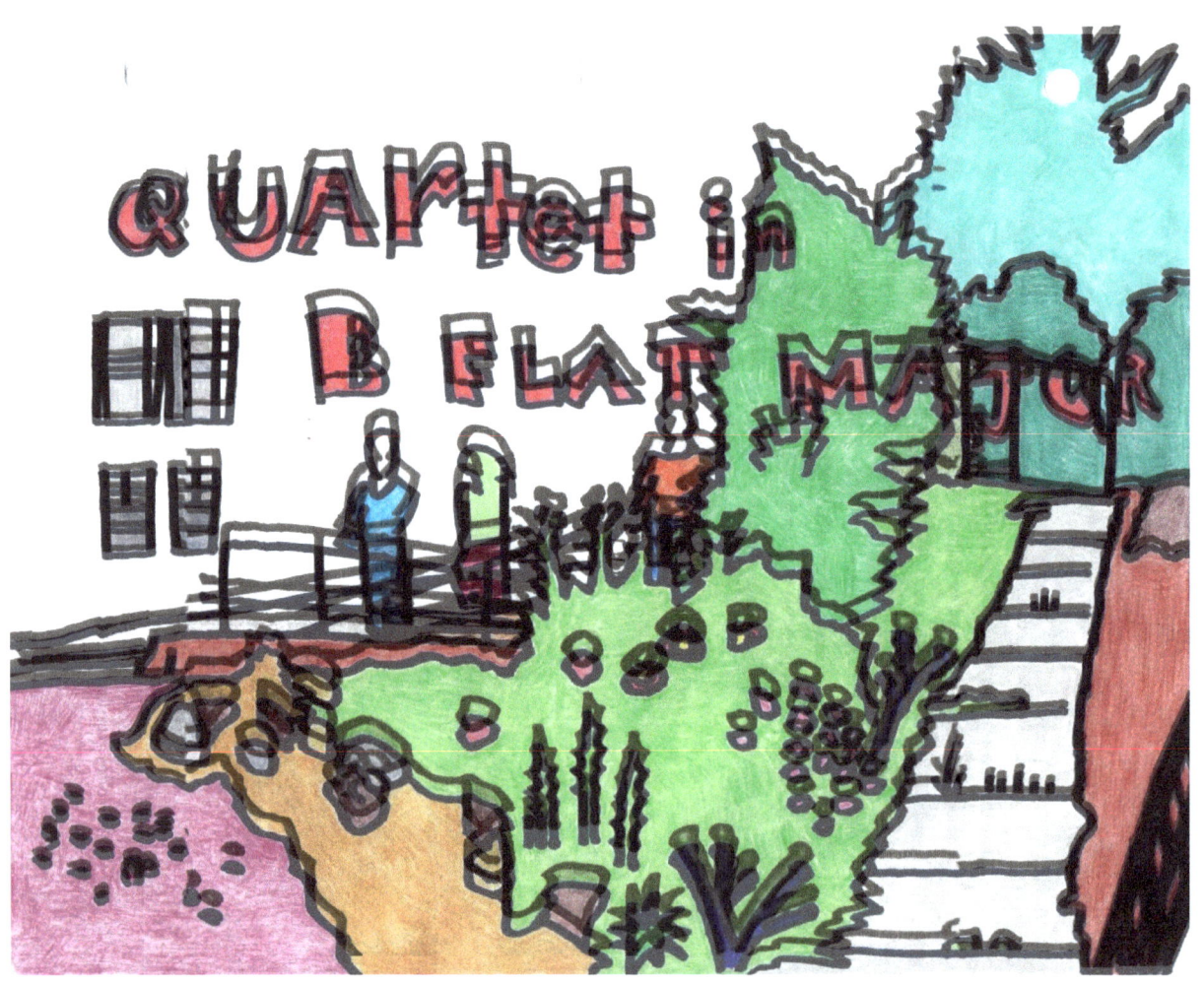

Quartet in B Flat Major / *UVM Campus, Burlington, VT*

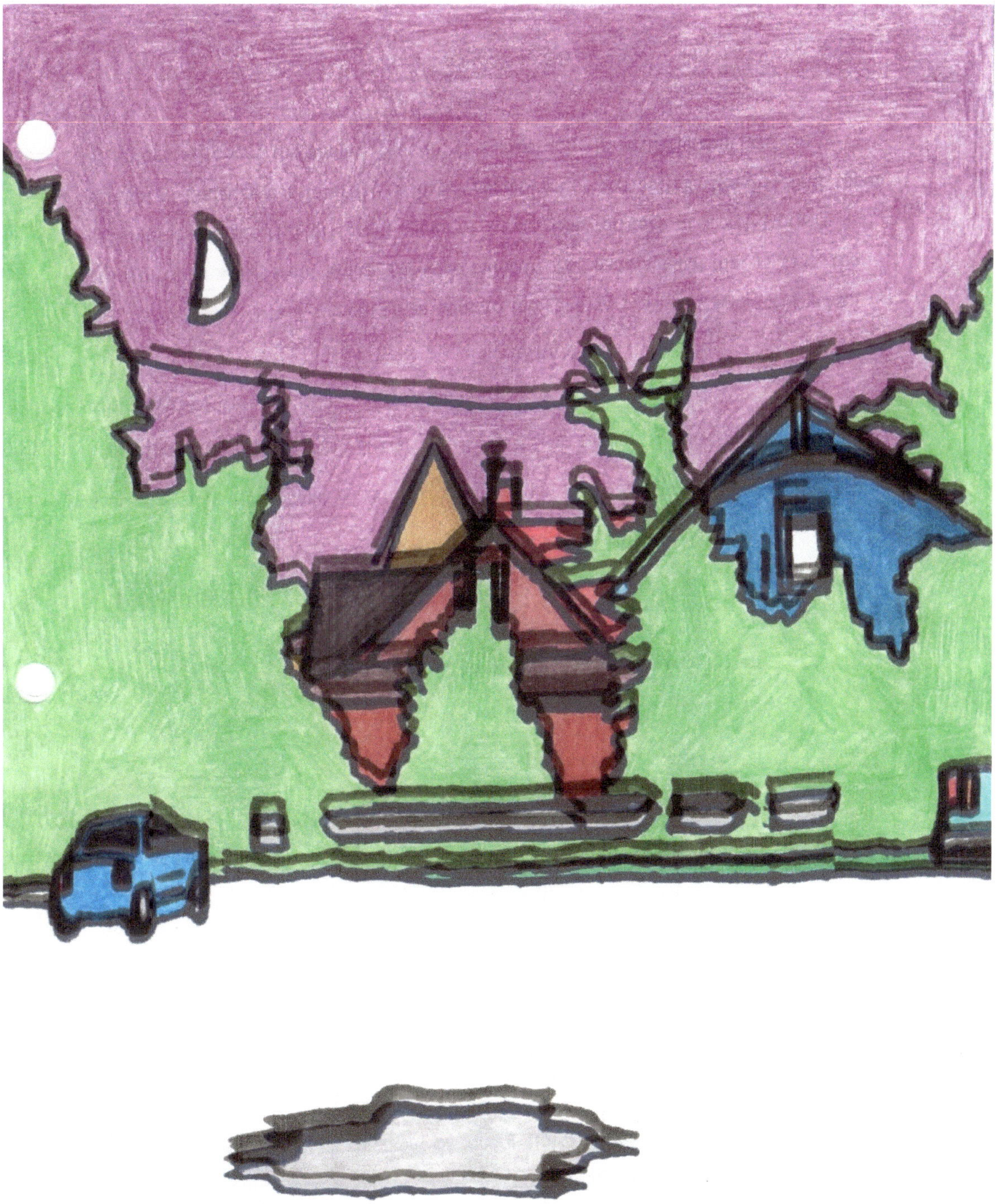

Untitled No. 1 // *Burlington, VT*

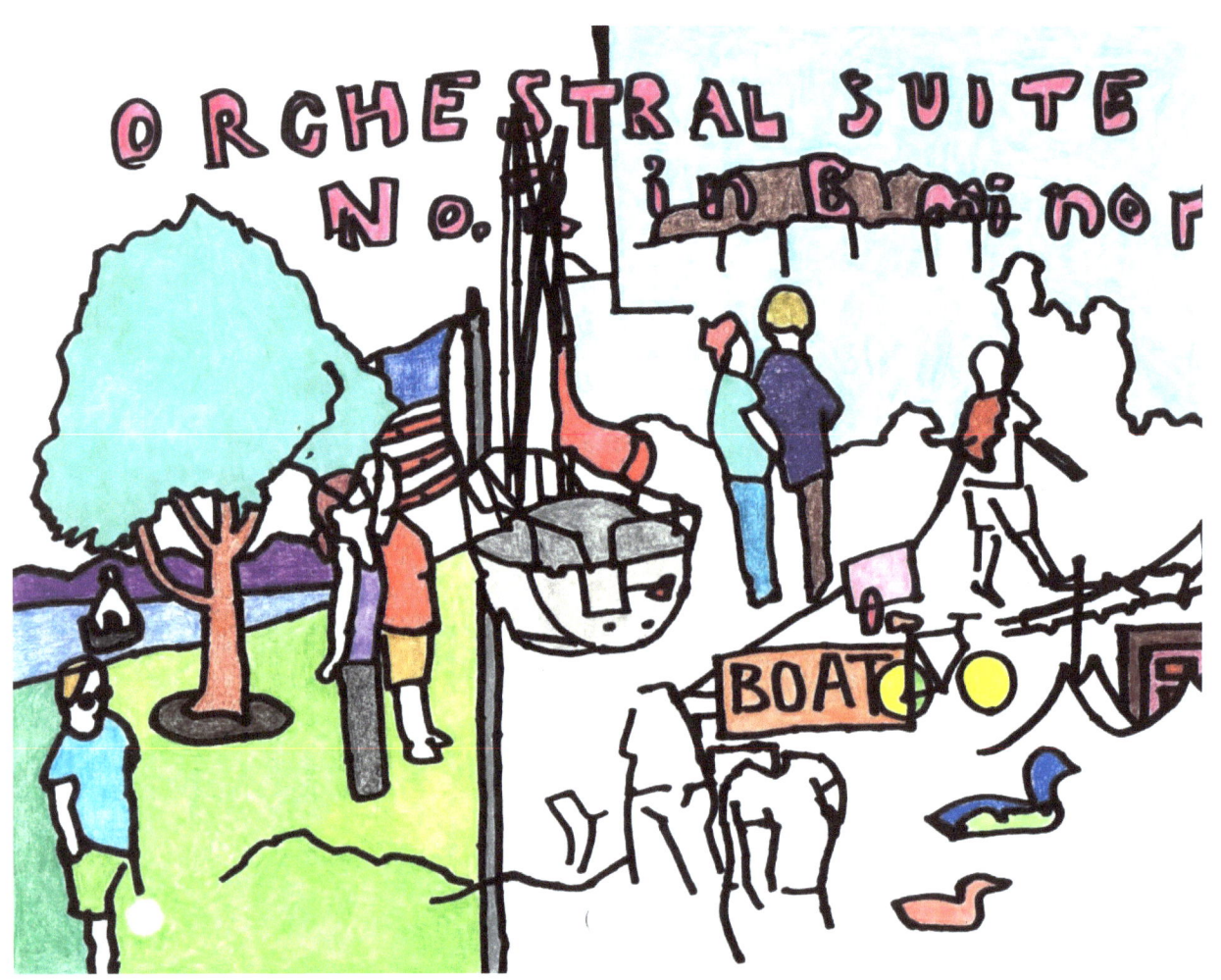

Waterfront Park No. 2 / *Burlington, VT*

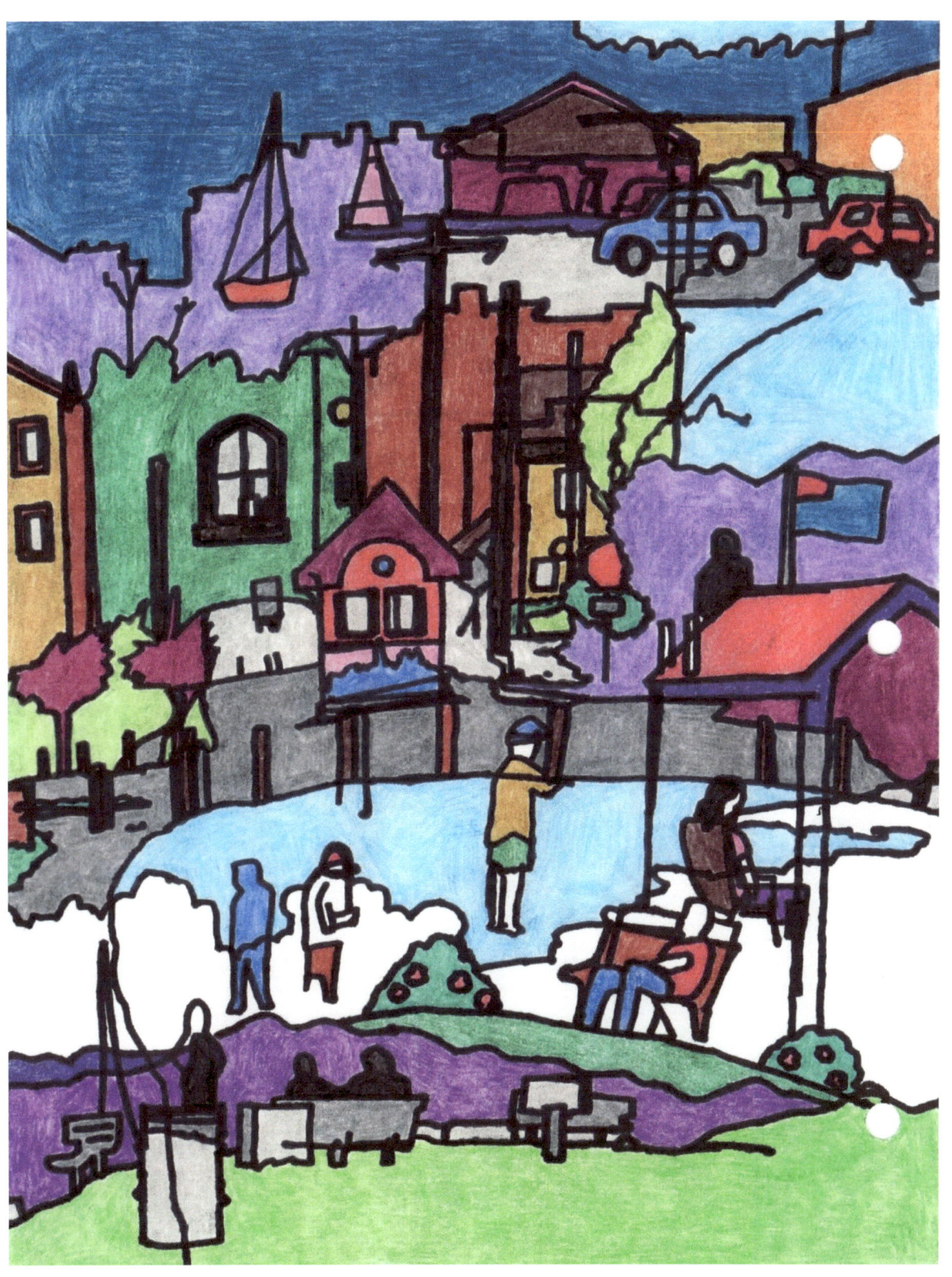

Perkins Pier / *Burlington, VT*

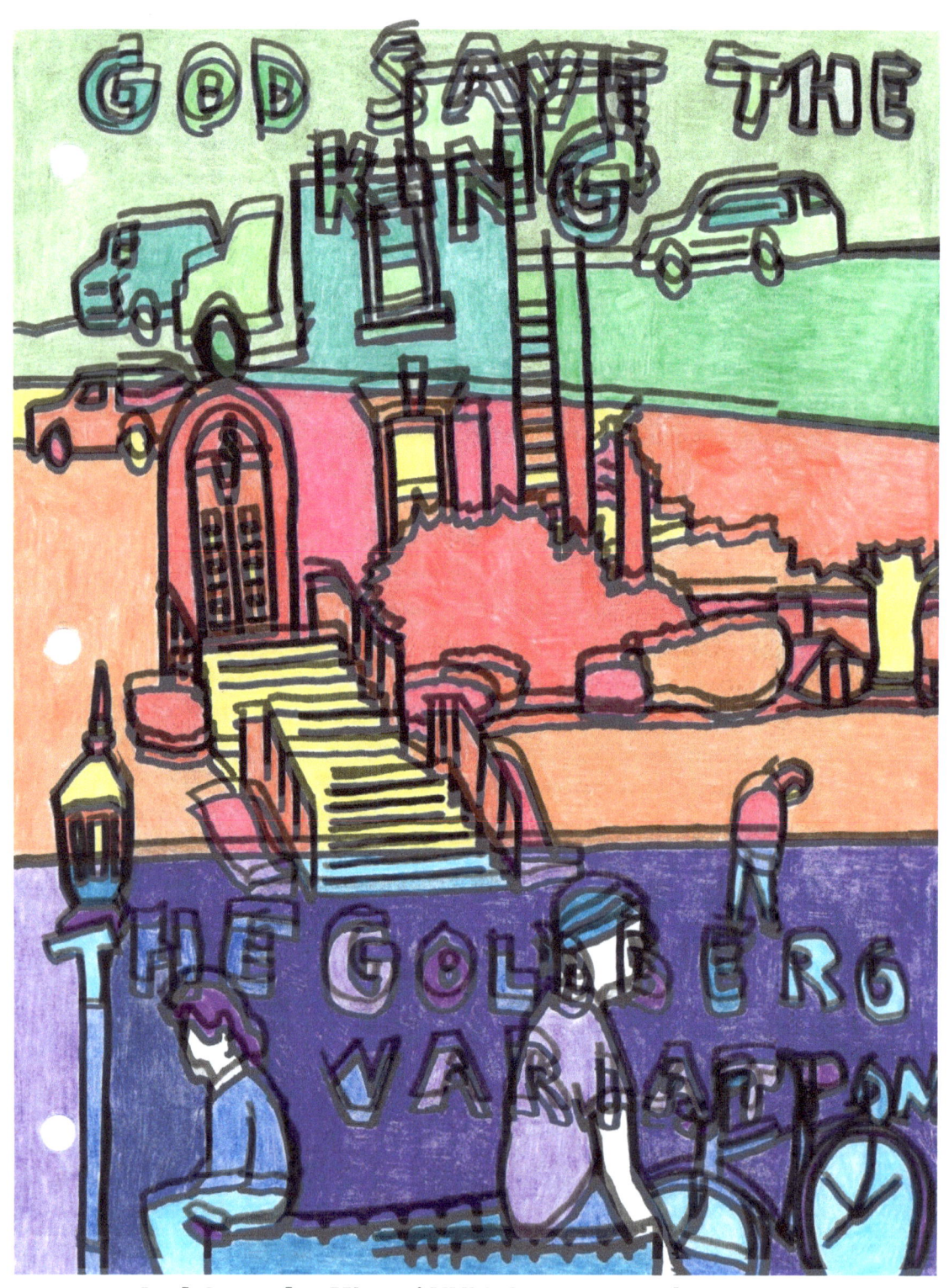

God Save the King / *UVM Campus, Burlington, VT*

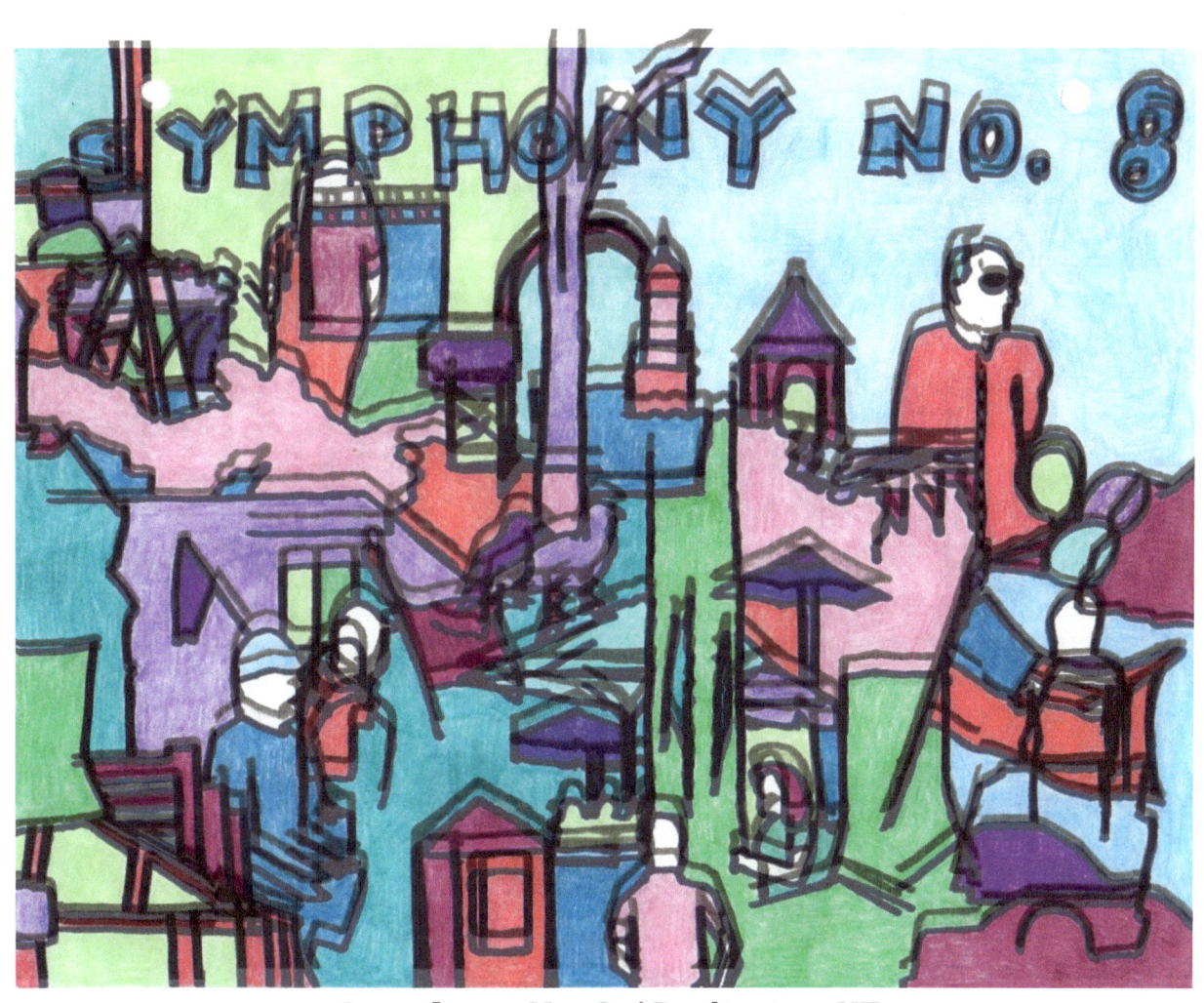

Symphony No: 8 / *Burlington, VT*

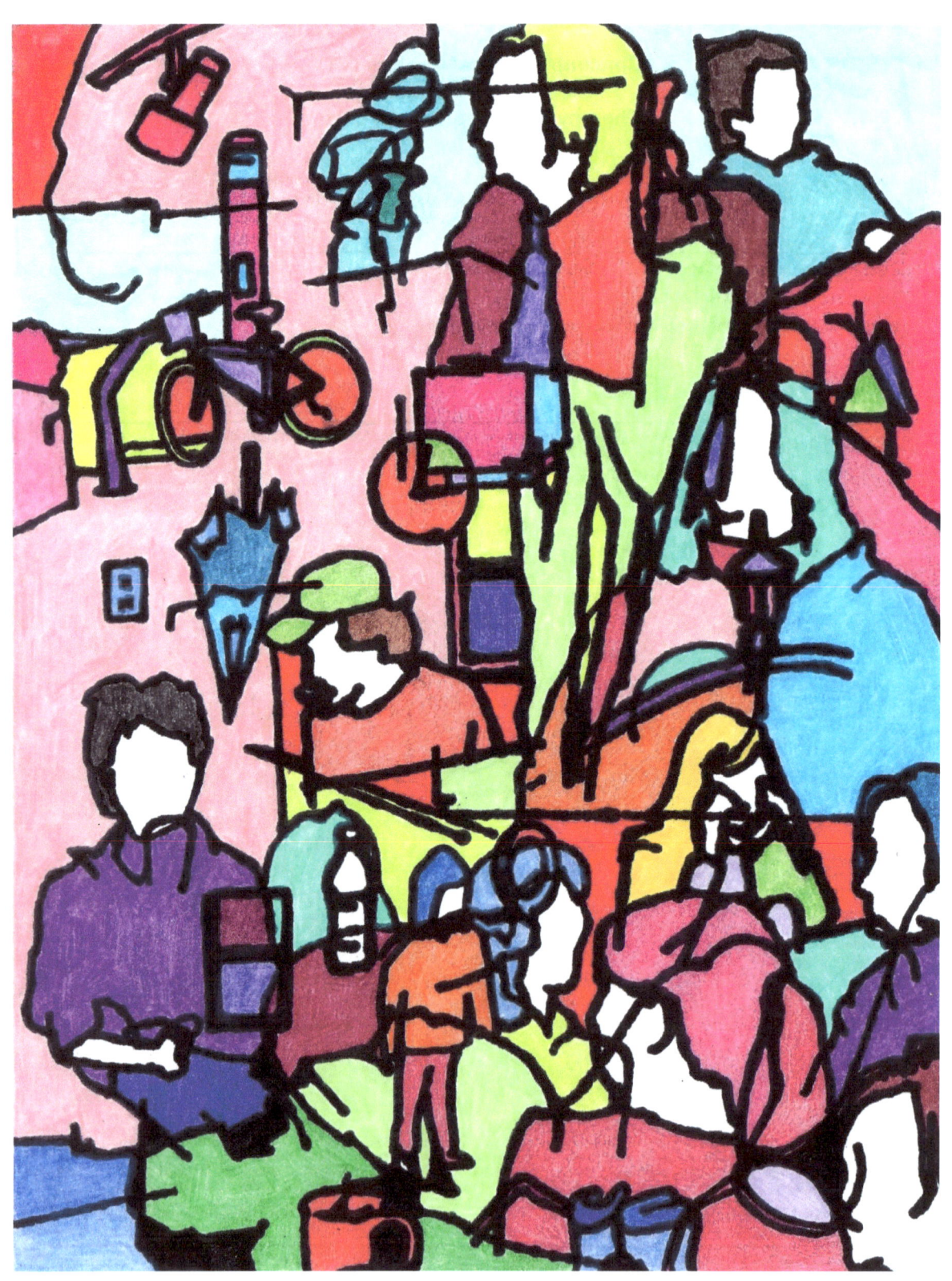

Untitled No. 2 / *Burlington, VT*

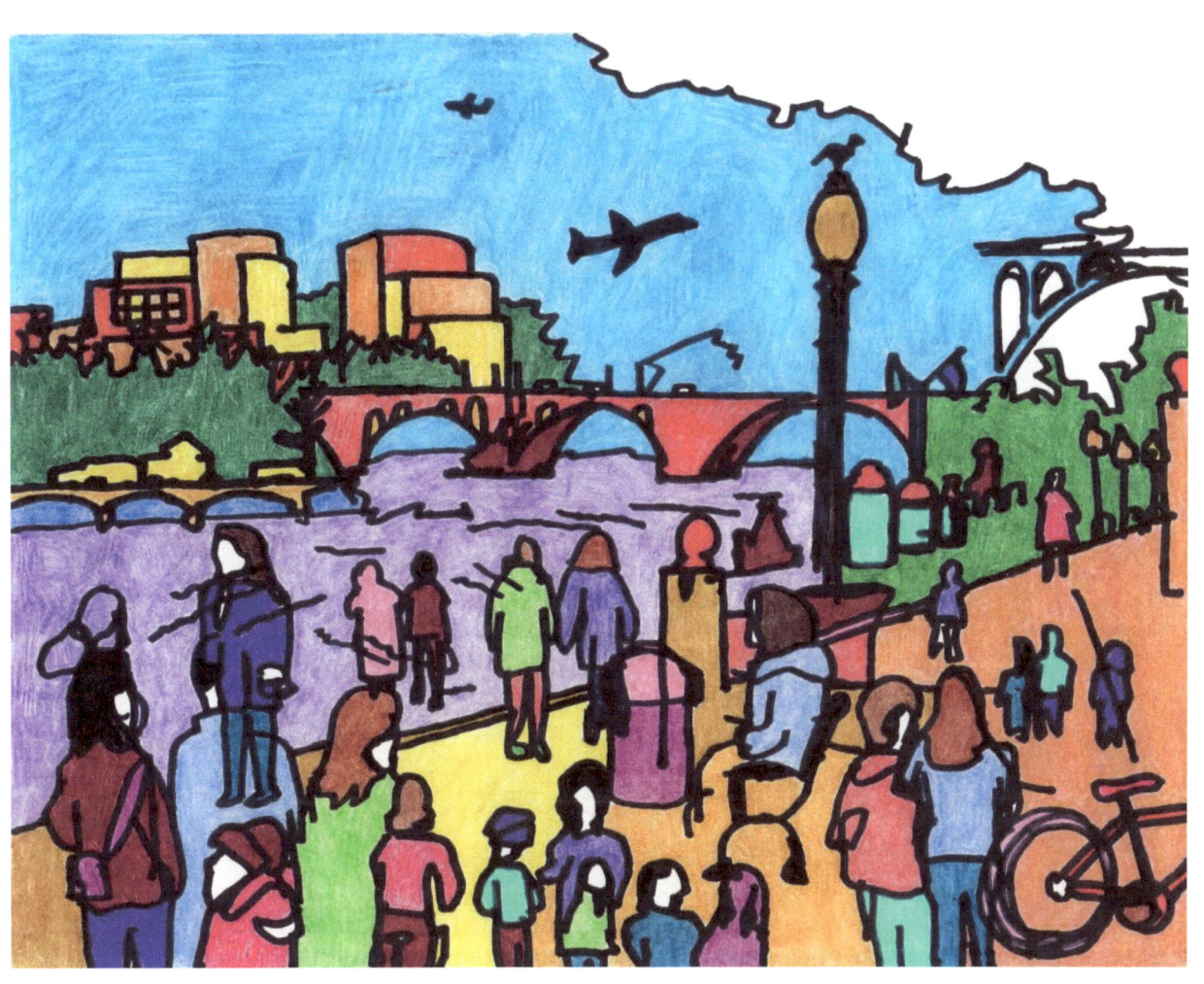

Georgetown / *Washington, DC*

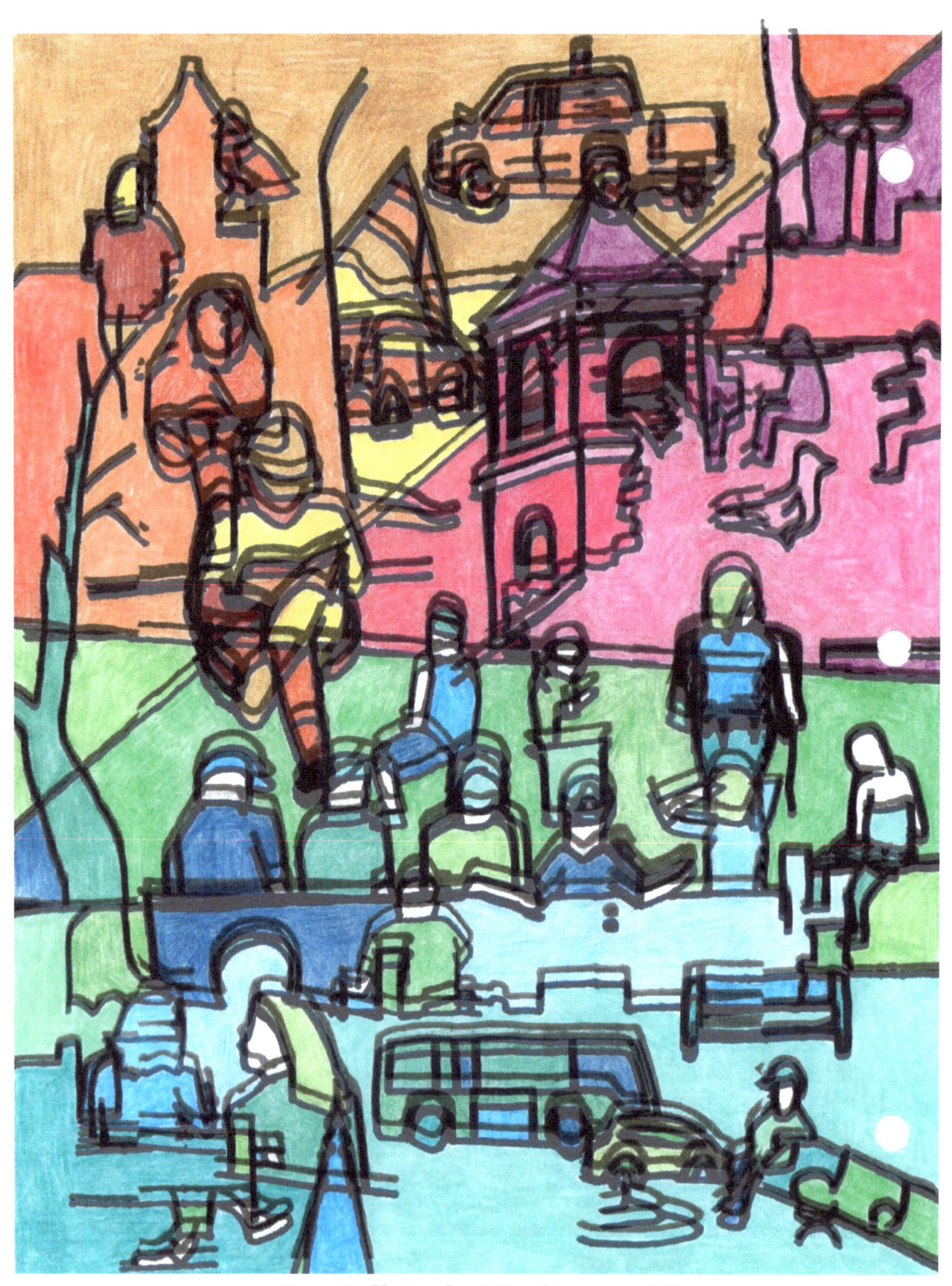

City Hall Park // Burlington, VT

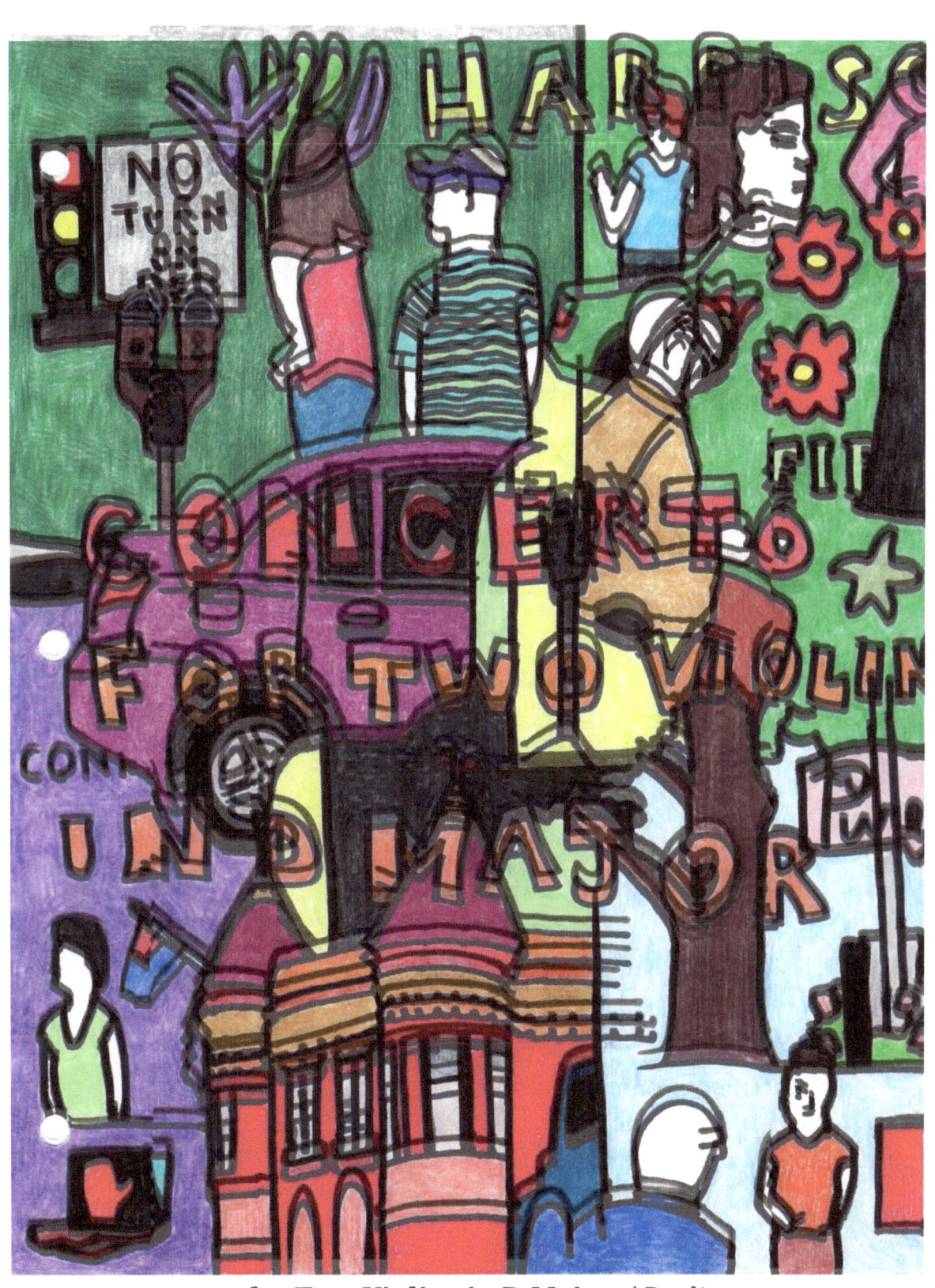

Concerto for Two Violins in D Major / *Burlington, VT*

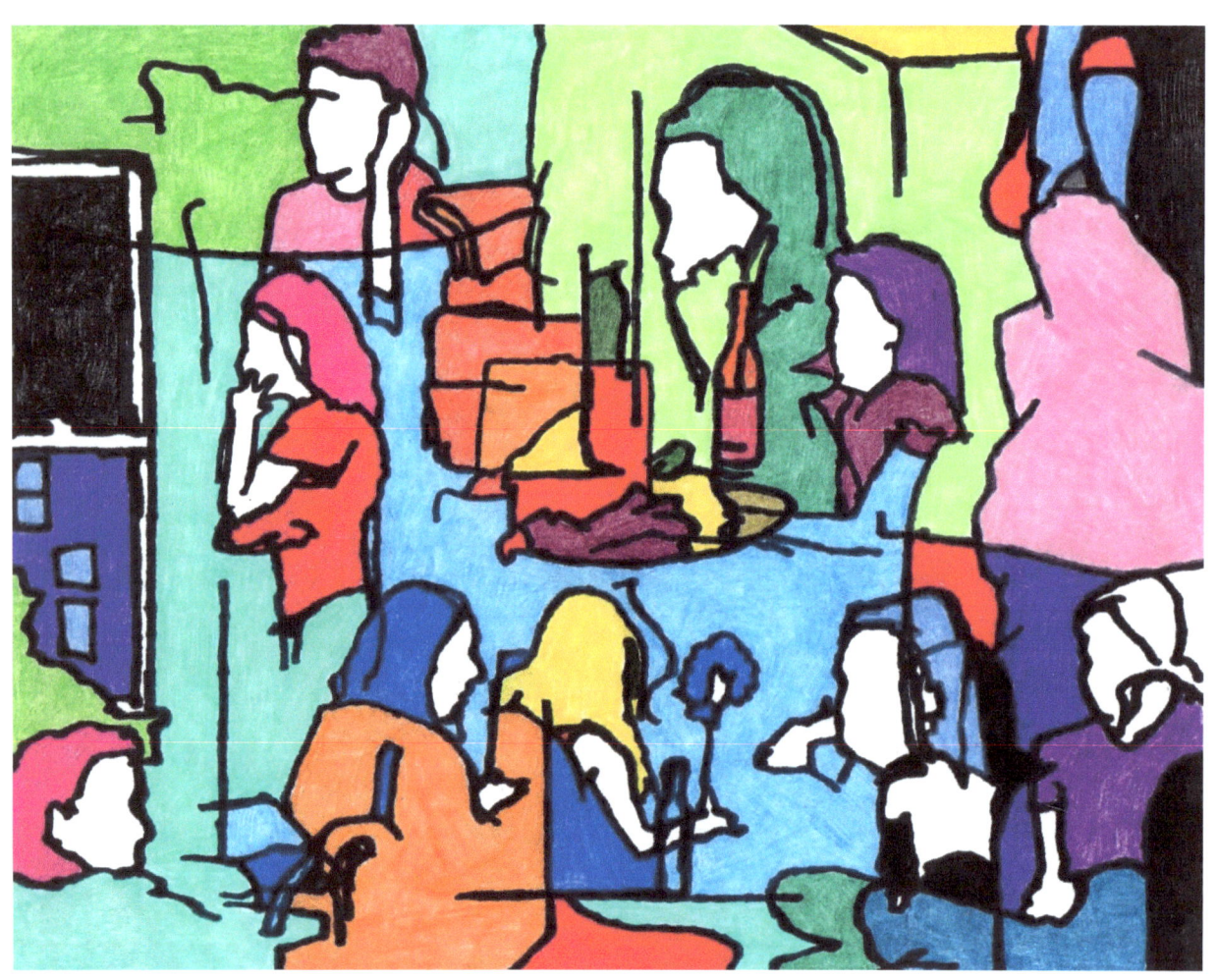

S.B. / Burlington, VT

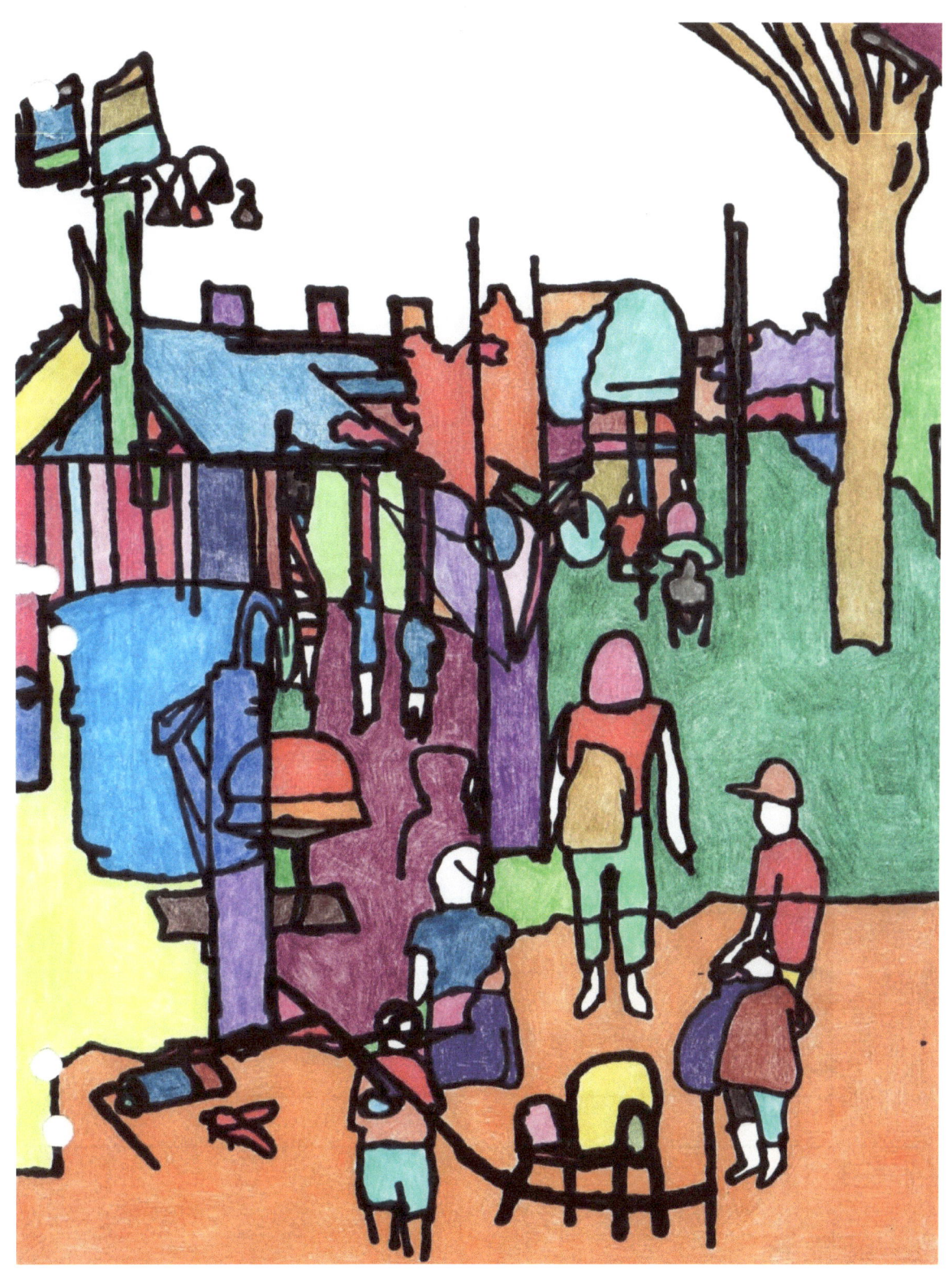

Church Street / *Burlington, VT*

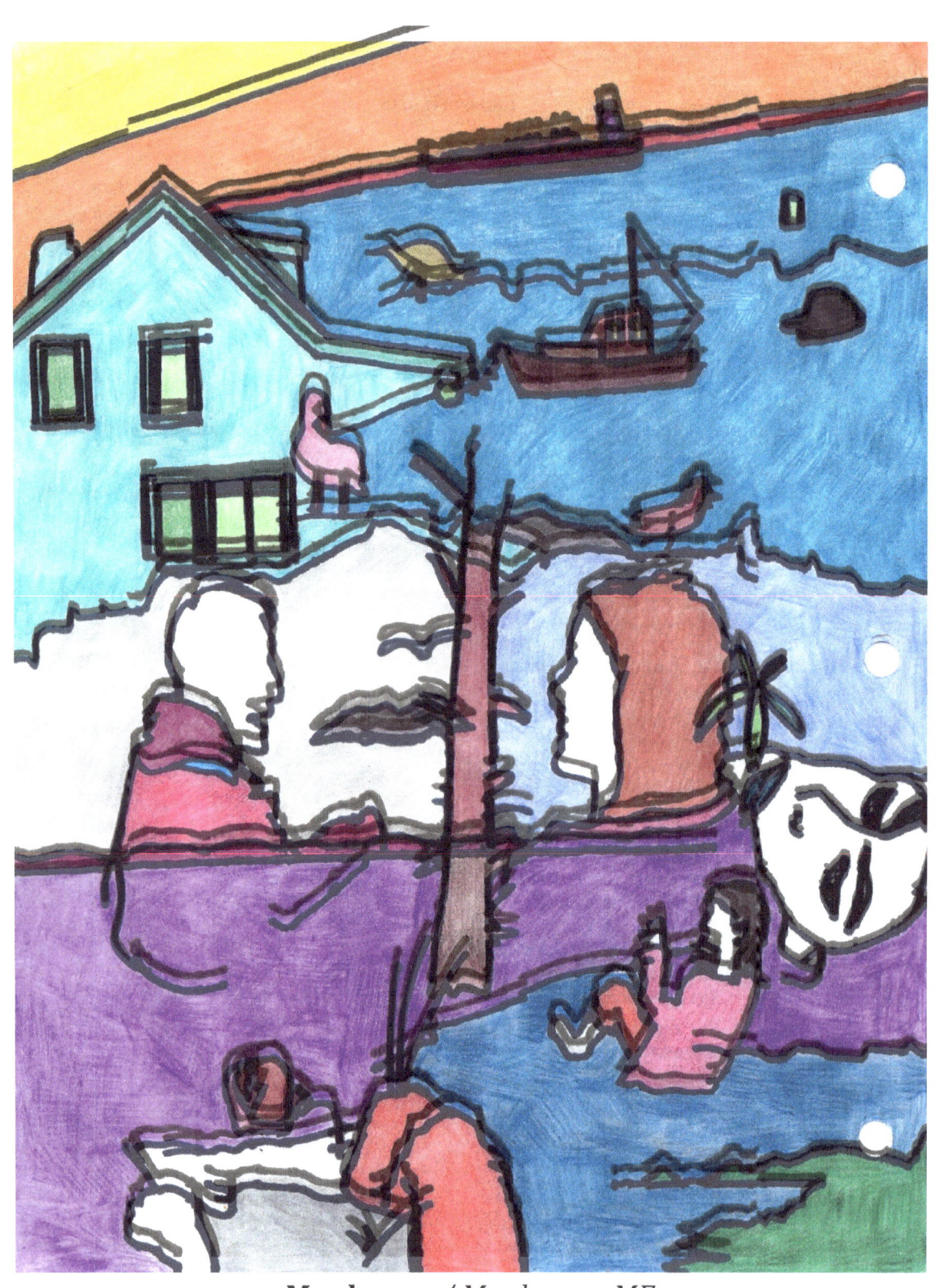

Monhegan / Monhegan, ME

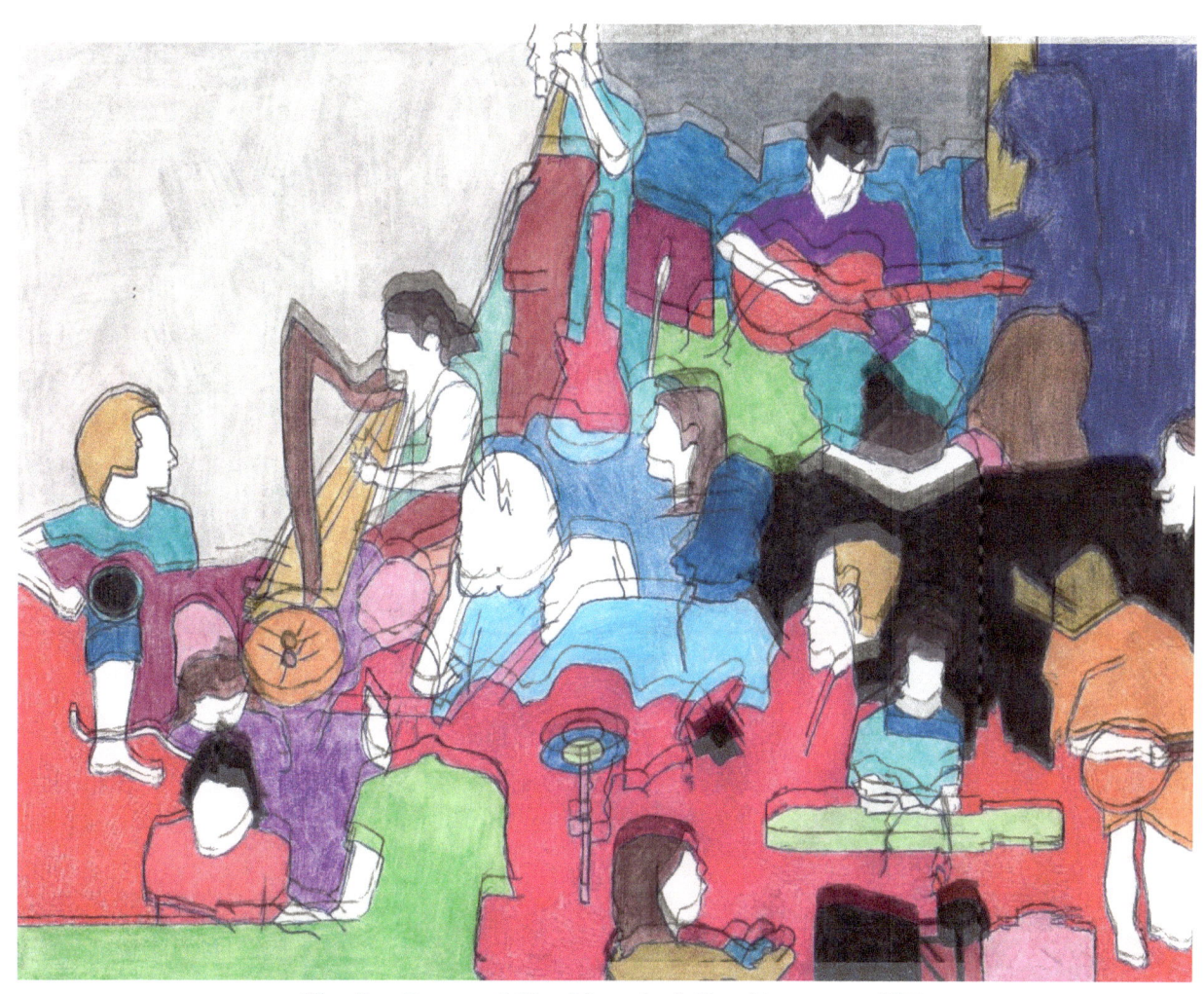

Slade Open Mic No. 1 // *Burlington, VT*

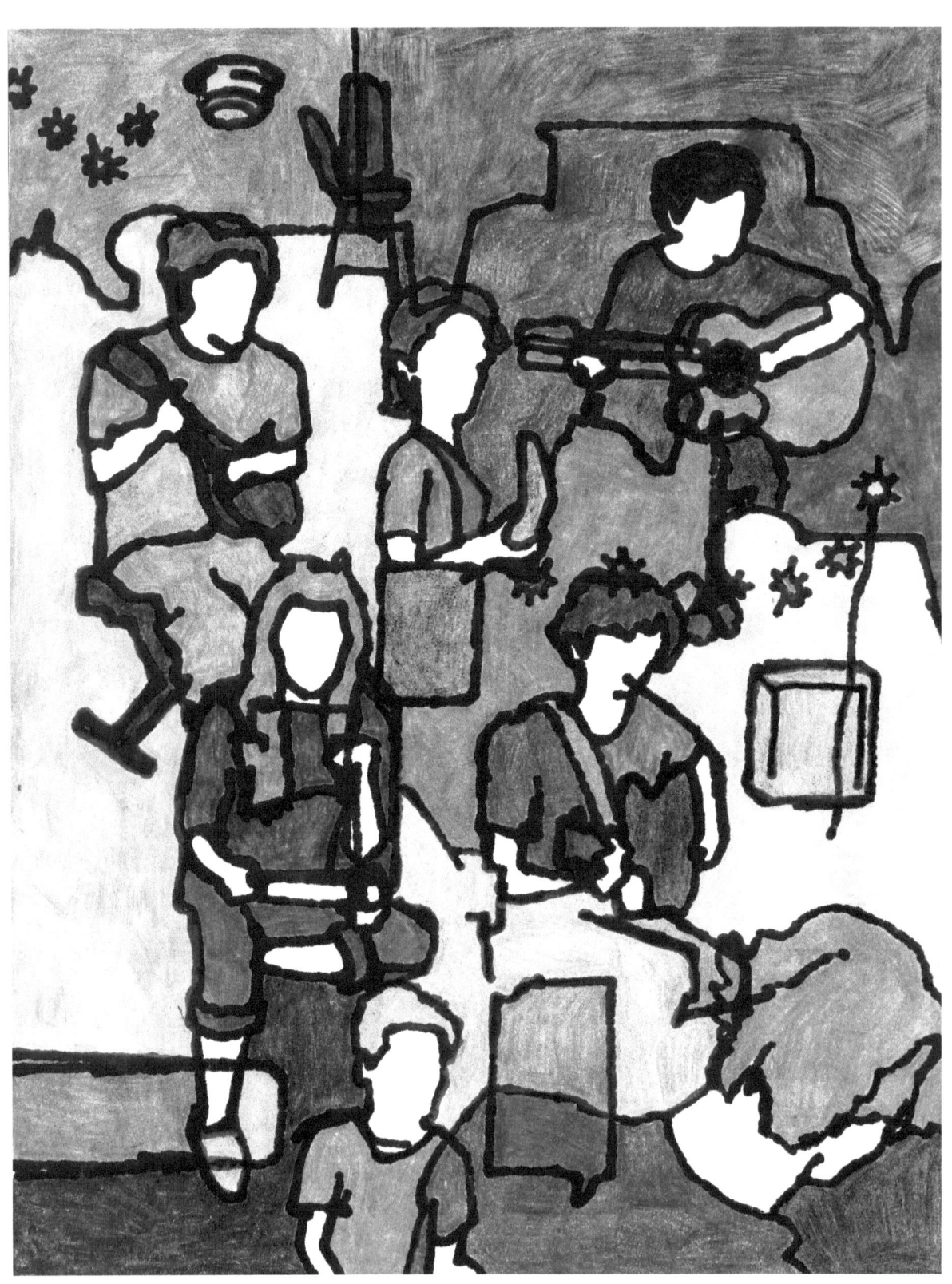

Slade Open Mic No. 2 (grayscale) / *Burlington, VT*

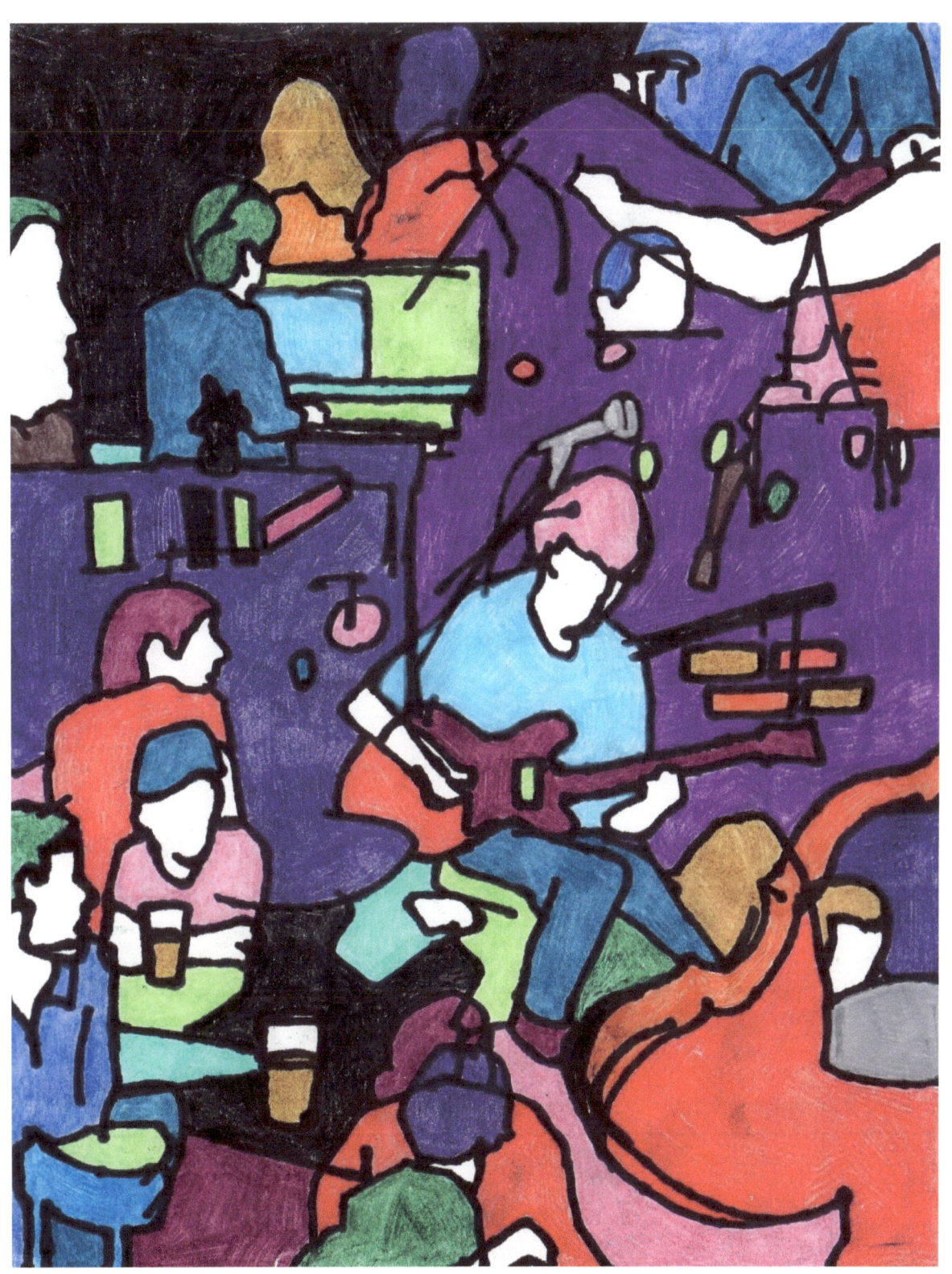

Radio Bean / *Burlington, VT*

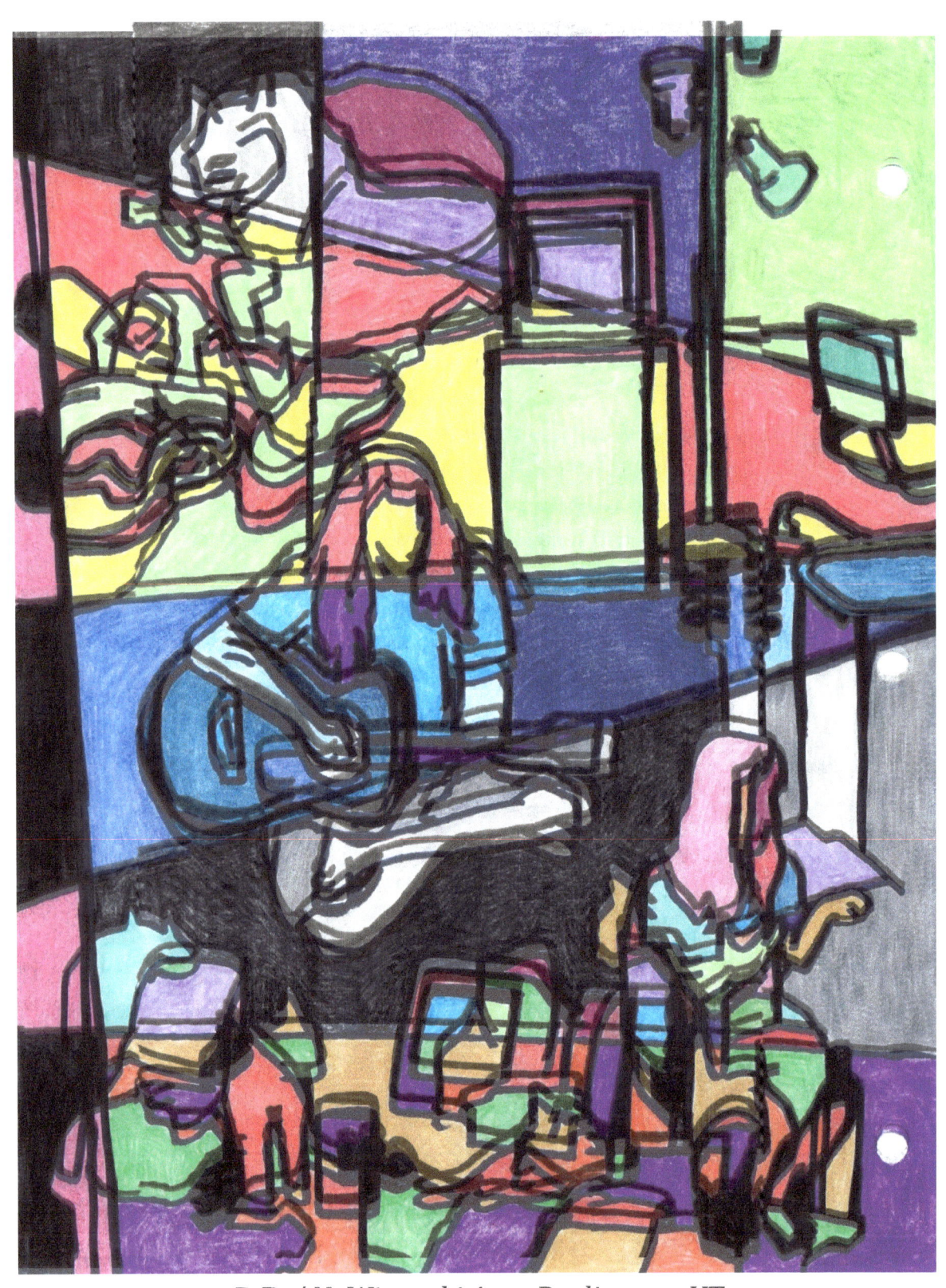

R.B. // N. Winooski Ave., Burlington, VT

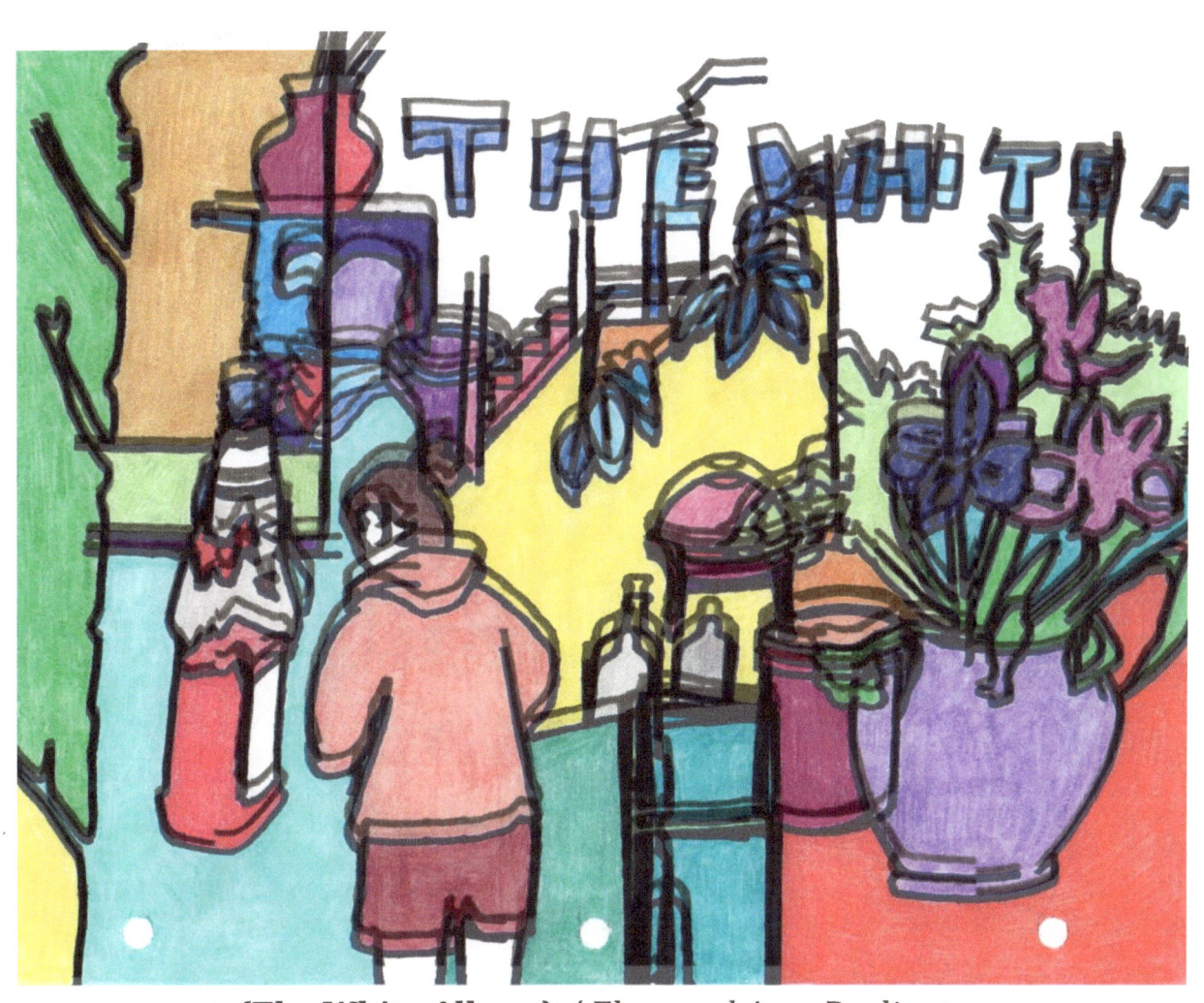

H.B. (The White Album) / Elmwood Ave., Burlington, VT

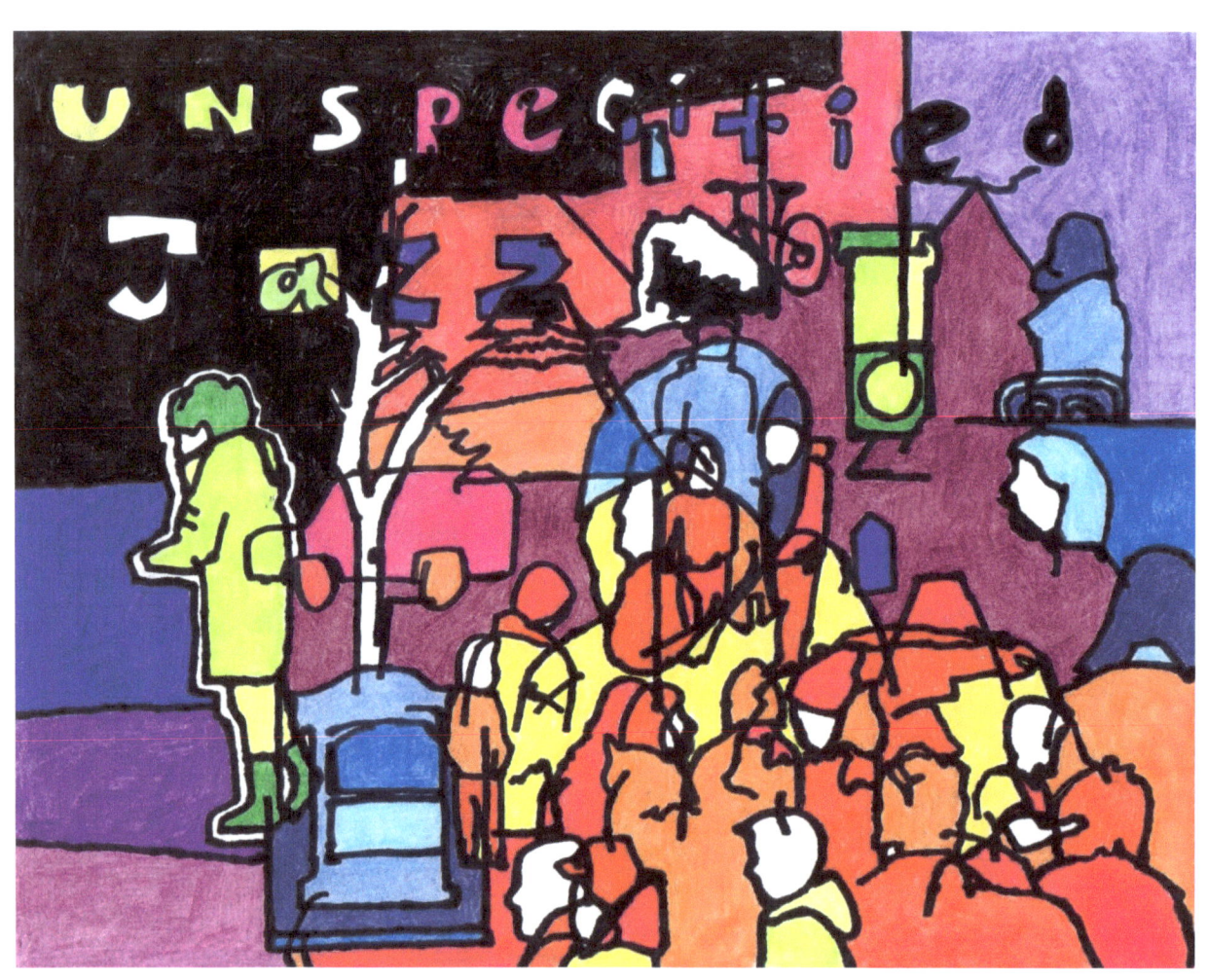

Uncommon Grounds / *Burlington, VT*

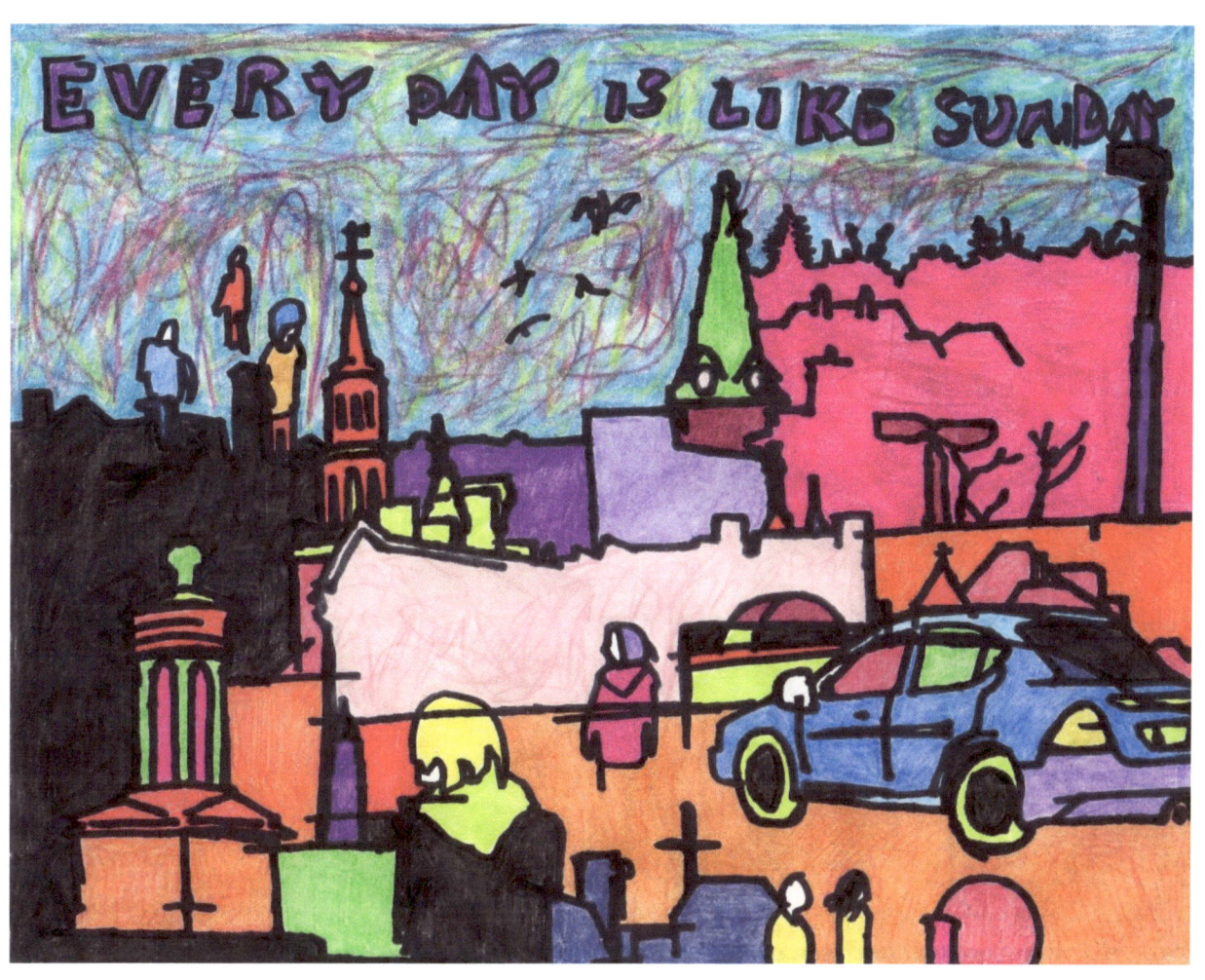

S. Winooski Ave. Parking Garage No. 2 / Burlington, VT

"I believe that the justification of art is the internal combustion it ignites in the hearts of men and not its shallow, externalized, public manifestations. The purpose of art is not the release of a momentary ejection of adrenaline but is, rather, the gradual, lifelong construction of a state of wonder and serenity."

— Glenn Gould

www.ingramcontent.com/pod-product-compliance
Lightning Source LLC
Chambersburg PA
CBHW051940210526
45473CB00006B/2316